Terrific TONGUES

Up Close

Enslow Elementary
an imprint of
Enslow Publishers, Inc.
40 Industrial Road
Box 398
Berkeley Heights, NJ 07922
USA

http://www.enslow.com

Melissa Stewart

CONTENTS

Words to Know   3

Alligator Snapping Turtle   4

Green Frog   6

Downy Woodpecker   8

Blue-Tongued Skink   10

Snake   12

Penguin   14

Cow   16

Your Tongue   18

Guessing Game   20

Learn More
  Books   22

  Web Sites   23

Index   24

WORDS TO KNOW

prey (PRAY)—An animal that is hunted by another animal.

sensor (SEN sur)—A tiny body part that detects sights, sounds, smells, tastes, or touches and sends messages to the brain.

ALLIGATOR SNAPPING TURTLE

Animals use their tongues in all kinds of ways. Take a look at this turtle's tongue! It looks just like a small, pink worm. And it wiggles like a worm, too.

When a hungry fish swims toward the tricky tongue, SNAP! The turtle gets a tasty meal.

4

GREEN FROG

Not all frogs have tongues, but a green frog does. Its tongue can strike faster than you can blink your eyes. A green frog's tongue is attached at the front of its mouth. That makes it easy to flip the tongue out, snatch some **prey**, and then curl the tongue back in.

DOWNY WOODPECKER

This bird's tongue is too long to fit in its mouth. It wraps around the bird's brain. The tongue protects the brain when the bird drills holes in trees. The long tongue is perfect for catching bugs that live deep inside trees.

8

BLUE-TONGUED SKINK

Can you guess what this lizard does when it feels scared? It opens its mouth and sticks out its tongue. That scares off most enemies.

SNAKE

A snake flicks its tongue in
and out. The tongue picks up tiny bits
in the air. Then the snake brushes the
bits against two holes on the top of its mouth.
The holes are full of **sensors** that help the snake
smell and taste.

PENGUIN

This bird's tongue is covered
with spikes. They point back toward
its throat. The spikes stop fish from sliding
out of the bird's mouth.

COW

A cow's tongue is long enough
to wash out her nose. She swallows all
the dirt, grime, and slippery slime. Yum!

YOUR TONGUE

You are an animal too. And you have a tongue. You use it to taste food. It also helps you eat and talk. You might even stick out your tongue when someone is mean to you.

GUESSING GAME

1. A gecko can use its tongue to . . .

2. A dog can use its tongue to . . .

3. An archerfish can use its tongue to . . .

4. A cat can use its tongue to . . .

A. shoot down prey with a stream of water

B. clean its eyes

C. cool its body on hot days

D. comb and smooth out its fur

Write your answers on a piece of paper. Please do not write in this book!

See answers on page 24.

gecko

dog

archerfish

cat

21

LEARN MORE

Books

Bozzo, Linda. *Amazing Animal Tongues*. New York: PowerKids Press, 2008.

Cusick, Dawn. *Animal Tongues*. Waynesville, N.C.: EarlyLight Books, 2009.

Jenkins, Steve and Robin Page. *What Do You Do With a Tail Like This?* Boston: Houghton Mifflin, 2003.

Randolph, Joanne. *Whose Tongue Is This?* New York: PowerKids Press, 2008.

WEB SITES

KidsHealth. *Your Tongue.*
<http://kidshealth.org/kid/
htbw/tongue.html>

Education.com.
Taste Test Science:
Fool Your Tongue!
<http://www.education.com/
activity/article/Taste_Test_
Science_Fool_Your>

INDEX

A

alligator snapping
   turtle, 4
archerfish, 20

B

blue-tongued skink, 10

C

cat, 20
cow, 16

D

dog, 20
downy woodpecker, 8

E

enemies, 10

F

fish, 14

G

garter snake, 12
gecko, 20
green frog, 6

H

human tongue, 18

P

penguin, 14
prey, 6, 20

S

sensor, 12

Note to Parents and Teachers: The Animal Bodies Up Close series supports the National Science Education Standards for K–4 science. The Words to Know section introduces subject-specific vocabulary words, including pronunciation and definitions. Early readers may need help with these new words.

Enslow Elementary, an imprint of Enslow Publishers, Inc.

Enslow Elementary® is a registered trademark of Enslow Publishers, Inc.

Copyright © 2012 by Melissa Stewart

All rights reserved.

No part of this book may be reproduced by any means without the written permission of the publisher.

Library of Congress Cataloging-in-Publication Data

Stewart, Melissa.

  Terrific tongues up close / Melissa Stewart.

    p. cm. — (Animal bodies up close)

  Includes index.

  Summary: "Discover how different animal use their tongues to clean themselves, capture food, and more"—Provided by publisher.

  ISBN 978-0-7660-3894-3

  1. Tongue—Juvenile literature. I. Title.

  QL946S74 2011

  573.3'57—dc22

              2011003341

Future editions:

Paperback ISBN 978-1-4644-0083-4

ePUB ISBN 978-1-4645-0990-2

PDF ISBN 978-1-4645-0990-9

Printed in China

012012 Leo Paper Group, Heshan City, Guangdong, China

10 9 8 7 6 5 4 3 2 1

To Our Readers: We have done our best to make sure all Internet Addresses in this book were active and appropriate when we went to press. However, the author and the publisher have no control over and assume no liability for the material available on those Internet sites or on other Web sites they may link to. Any comments or suggestions can be sent by e-mail to comments@enslow.com or to the address on the back cover.

Photo Credits: © 2011 Photos.com, a division of Getty Images, pp. 18, 19, 21 (dog); © Ardea/Watson, M./Animals Animals - Earth Scenes, p. 8; George Grall/National Geographic Stock, p. 4; © Lockwood, C.C./Animals Animals - Earth Scenes, p. 5; Minden Pictures: © Mitsuaki Iwago, p. 11, © Stephen Dalton, p. 7; Photolibrary: © Bios, p. 14, © Peter Arnold Images, pp. 6, 15; Photo Researchers, Inc.: © Gary Meszaros, p. 3 (prey), © John Mitchell, pp. 3 (sensor), 12, © Stephen Dalton, p. 21 (archerfish); Shutterstock.com, pp. 1, 2, 10, 16, 17, 21 (gecko, cat), 23; © Steve Byland/Dreamstime.com, p. 13; Thomas Hays, p. 9.

Cover Photo: Shutterstock.com

Series Literacy Consultant:
Allan A. De Fina, PhD
Dean, College of Education
Professor of Literacy Education
New Jersey City University
Past President of the New Jersey Reading
  Association

Science Consultant:
Helen Hess, PhD
Professor of Biology
College of the Atlantic
Bar Harbor, Maine

Answers to the Guessing Game

1. Gecko: B, clean its eyes
2. Dog: C, cool its body on hot days
3. Archerfish: A, shoot down prey with a stream of w...
4. Cat: D, comb and smooth out its fur